OCA/OCP – STUDY GUIDE 1Z0-147

OCA/OCP –PL/SQL

ORACLE CERTIFICATION EXAM

SOLVED QUESTIONS & ANSWERS

WITH

EXPLANATION

1. Examine this function:

   CREATE OR REPLACE FUNCTION CALC_PLAYER_AVG

   (V_ID in PLAYER_BAT_STAT.PLAYER_ID%TYPE) RETURN NUMBER

   IS

   V_AVG NUMBER;

   BEGIN

   SELECT HITS / AT_BATS INTO V_AVG

   FROM PLAYER_BAT_STAT WHERE PLAYER_ID = V_ID; RETURN (V_AVG);

   END;

   Which statement will successfully invoke this function in SQL *Plus?

   A. SELECT CALC_PLAYER_AVG(PLAYER_ID) FROM PLAYER_BAT_STAT;
   B. EXECUTE CALC_PLAYER_AVG(31);
   C. CALC_PLAYER('RUTH');
   D. CALC_PLAYER_AVG(31);
   E. START CALC_PLAYER_AVG(31)

   Answer: A

   Explanation:

   A function can be invoked in SELECT Statement provided that the function does not modify any database tables. The function must use positional notation to pass values to the formal parameters. The formal parameters must be of the IN mode. They should return data types acceptable to SQL and they should not include any transaction, session, or system control statements.

   Also, you can't call a function in the way mentioned in other options B to E, because function must return a value, to call a function using EXECUTE command you should declare a bind variable using the VARIABLE command then assign the value returned from the function to this variable, in the following way:

   SQL> VARIABLE v_get_value NUMBER

   SQL> EXECUTE: v_get_value := CALC_PLAYER_AVG(31)

   PL/SQL procedure successfully completed.

   SQL> PRINT v_get_value V_GET_VALUE

2. Which three are true statements about dependent objects? (Choose three)

A. Invalid objects cannot be described.
B. An object with status of invalid cannot be a referenced object.
C. The Oracle server automatically records dependencies among objects.
D. All schema objects have a status that is recorded in the data dictionary.
E. You can view whether an object is valid or invalid in the USER_STATUS data dictionary view.
F. You can view whether an object is valid or invalid in the USER_OBJECTS data dictionary view.

Answer: A, C, F

3. You have created a stored procedure DELETE_TEMP_TABLE that uses dynamic SQL to remove a table in your schema. You have granted the EXECUTE privilege to user A on this procedure. When user A executes the DELETE_TEMP_TABLE procedure, under whose privileges are the operations performed by default?

A. SYS privileges
B. Your privileges
C. Public privileges
D. User A's privileges
E. User A cannot execute your procedure that has dynamic SQL.

Answer: B

4. Examine this code:

CREATE OR REPLACE PRODECURE add_dept

(p_dept_name VARCHAR2 DEFAULT 'placeholder', p_location VARCHAR2 DEFAULT 'Boston')

IS BEGIN

INSERT INTO departments

VALUES (dept_id_seq.NEXTVAL, p_dept_name, p_location); END add_dept;

/

Which three are valid calls to the add_dep procedure? (Choose three)

A. add_dept;
B. add_dept('Accounting');
C. add_dept(, 'New York');
D. add_dept(p_location=>'New York');

Answer: A, B, D

5. Which two statements about packages are true? (Choose two)

A. Packages can be nested.
B. You can pass parameters to packages.
C. A package is loaded into memory each time it is invoked.
D. The contents of packages can be shared by many applications.
E. You can achieve information hiding by making package constructs private.

Answer: D, E

Explanation:

Actually these are some of the advantages of the package, sharing the package among applications and hide the logic of the procedures and function that are inside the package by declaring them in the package header and write the code of these procedures and functions inside the package body.

6. Which two programming constructs can be grouped within a package? (Choose two)

A. Cursor
B. Constant
C. Trigger
D. Sequence
E. View

Answer: A, B

Explanation:

The constructs that can be grouped within a package include: Procedures and Functions, Cursors, Variables and Constants, Composite data types such as TABLE or RECORD, Exceptions, Comments, PRAGMAs.

7. Which two statements describe the state of a package variable after executing the package in which it is declared? (Choose two)

A. It persists across transactions within a session.
B. It persists from session to session for the same user.
C. It does not persist across transaction within a session.
D. It persists from user to user when the package is invoked.
E. It does not persist from session to session for the same user.

Answer: A, E

8. Which code can you use to ensure that the salary is not increased by more than 10% at a time nor is it ever decreased?

A. ALTER TABLE emp ADD

CONSTRAINT ck_sal CHECK (sal BETWEEN sal AND sal*1.1);

B. CREATE OR REPLACE TRIGGER check_sal BEFORE UPDATE OF sal ON emp

FOR EACH ROW

WHEN (new.sal < old.sal OR new.sal > old.sal * 1.1) BEGIN

RAISE_APPLICATION_ERROR (- 20508, 'Do not decrease salary not increase by more than 10 %');

END;

C. CREATE OR REPLACE TRIGGER check_sal BEFORE UPDATE OF sal ON emp

WHEN (new.sal < old.sal OR new.sal > old.sal * 1.1) BEGIN

RAISE_APPLICATION_ERROR (- 20508, 'Do not decrease salary not increase by more than 10 %');

END;

D. CREATE OR REPLACE TRIGGER check_sal AFTER UPDATE OR sal ON emp

WHEN (new.sal < old.sal OR -new.sal > old.sal * 1.1) BEGIN

RAISE_APPLICATION_ERROR (- 20508, 'Do not decrease salary not increase by more than 10%');

END;

Answer: B

Explanation:

Row triggers are the correct chose for solving the problem. A row trigger fires each time the table is affected by the triggering event. If the triggering event affects no rows, a row trigger is not executed.

Row triggers are useful if the trigger action depends on data of rows that are affected or on data provided by the triggering event itself. You can create a

BEFORE row trigger in order to prevent the triggering operation from succeeding if a certain condition is violated.

Within a ROW trigger, reference the value of a column before and after the data change by prefixing it with the OLD and NEW qualifier.

9. Examine this code:

```
CREATE OR REPLACE PACKAGE bonus IS

g_max_bonus NUMBER := .99;

FUNCTION calc_bonus (p_emp_id NUMBER) RETURN NUMBER;

FUNCTION calc_salary (p_emp_id NUMBER) RETURN NUMBER;

END;

/

CREATE OR REPLACE PACKAGE BODY bonus IS

v_salary employees.salary%TYPE;

v_bonus employees.commission_pct%TYPE; FUNCTION calc_bonus
(p_emp_id NUMBER) RETURN NUMBER

IS BEGIN

SELECT salary, commission_pct INTO v_salary, v_bonus

FROM employees

WHERE employee_id = p_emp_id; RETURN v_bonus * v_salary; END
calc_bonus

FUNCTION calc_salary (p_emp_id NUMBER) RETURN NUMBER

IS BEGIN

SELECT salary, commission_pct INTO v_salary, v_bonus

FROM employees WHERE employees


RETURN v_bonus * v_salary + v_salary; END cacl_salary;

END bonus;

/
```

Which statement is true?

A. You can call the BONUS.CALC_SALARY packaged function from an INSERT command against the EMPLOYEES table.
B. You can call the BONUS.CALC_SALARY packaged function from a SELECT command against the EMPLOYEES table.
C. You can call the BONUS.CALC_SALARY packaged function form a DELETE command against the EMPLOYEES table.
D. You can call the BONUS.CALC_SALARY packaged function from an UPDATE command against the EMPLOYEES table.

Answer: B

10. Which statement is valid when removing procedures?

A. Use a drop procedure statement to drop a standalone procedure.
B. Use a drop procedure statement to drop a procedure that is part of a package. Then recompile the package specification.
C. Use a drop procedure statement to drop a procedure that is part of a package. Then recompile the package body.
D. For faster removal and re-creation, do not use a drop procedure statement. Instead, recompile the procedure using the alter procedure statement with the REUSE SETTINGS clause.

Answer: A

Explanation:

The DROP DROCEDURE statement is used to drop a standalone procedure

11. Examine this package:

CREATE OR REPLACE PACKAGE BB_PACK IS

V_MAX_TEAM_SALARY NUMBER(12,2);

PROCEDURE ADD_PLAYER(V_ID IN NUMBER, V_LAST_NAME VARCHAR2, NUMBER);

END BB_PACK;

/

CREATE OR REPLACE PACKAGE BODY BB_PACK IS

PROCEDURE UPD_PLAYER_STAT

(V_ID IN NUMBER, V_AB IN NUMBER DEFAULT 4, V_HITS IN NUMBER)

IS BEGIN

UPDATE PLAYER_BAT_STAT

SET AT_BATS = AT_BATS + V_AB, HITS = HITS + V_HITS

WHERE PLAYER_ID = V_ID; COMMIT;

END UPD_PLAYER_STAT;

PROCEDURE ADD_PLAYER

(V_ID IN NUMBER, V_LAST_NAME VARCHAR2, V_SALARY NUMBER) IS

BEGIN

INSERT INTO PLAYER(ID,LAST_NAME,SALARY) VALUES (V_ID, V_LAST_NAME, V_SALARY);

UPD_PLAYER_STAT(V_ID,0,0); END ADD_PLAYER;

END BB_PACK;

You make a change to the body of the BB_PACK package. The BB_PACK body is recompiled.

What happens if the stand alone procedure VALIDATE_PLAYER_STAT references this package?

A. VALIDATE_PLAYER_STAT cannot recompile and must be recreated.
B. VALIDATE_PLAYER_STAT is not invalidated.
C. VALIDATE_PLAYER_STAT is invalidated.
D. VALIDATE_PLAYER_STAT and BB_PACK are invalidated.

Answer: B

Explanation:

You can greatly simplify dependency management with packages when referencing a package procedure or function from a stand-alone procedure or function.

If the package body changes and the package specification does not change, the stand-alone procedure referencing a package construct remains valid.

If the package specification changes, the outside procedure referencing a package construct is invalidated, as is the package body.

12. You need to create a trigger on the EMP table that monitors every row that is changed and places this information into the AUDIT_TABLE.

What type of trigger do you create?

A. FOR EACH ROW trigger on the EMP table.
B. Statement-level trigger on the EMP table.
C. FOR EACH ROW trigger on the AUDIT_TABLE table.
D. Statement-level trigger on the AUDIT_TABLE table.
E. FOR EACH ROW statement-level trigger on the EMP table.

Answer: A

Explanation:

A FOR EACH ROW trigger on the EMP table will fire for each row that is modified in the employee table and will insert a record in the AUDIT_TABLE for each corresponding row modified in the EMP Table. A Statement-level trigger will only fire once and could only be used to insert a single row into the AUTIT_TABLE.

13. Which statements are true? (Choose all that apply)

A. If errors occur during the compilation of a trigger, the trigger is still created.
B. If errors occur during the compilation of a trigger you can go into SQL *Plus and query the USER_TRIGGERS data dictionary view to see the compilation errors.
C. If errors occur during the compilation of a trigger you can use the SHOW ERRORS command within iSQL *Plus to see the compilation errors.
D. If errors occur during the compilation of a trigger you can go into SQL *Plus and query the USER_ERRORS data dictionary view to see compilation errors.

Answer: A, C, D

14. Which two dictionary views track dependencies? (Choose two)

A. USER_SOURCE
B. UTL_DEPTREE
C. USER_OBJECTS
D. DEPTREE_TEMPTAB

E. USER_DEPENDENCIES
F. DBA_DEPENDENT_OBJECTS

Answer: D, E

Explanation:
DEPTREE_TEMPTAB is a temporary table used to store dependency information returned by the DEPTREE_FILL procedure. USER_DEPENDECIES is used to display direct dependencies. ALL_DEPENDENCIES and DBA_DEPENDENCIES also store dependency information.

15. Given a function CALCTAX:

CREATE OR REPLACE FUNCTION calctax (sal NUMBER) RETURN NUMBER

IS BEGIN

RETURN (sal * 0.05); END;

If you want to run the above function from the SQL *Plus prompt, which statement is true?

A. You need to execute the command CALCTAX (1000);.
B. You need to execute the command EXECUTE FUNCTION calctax;
C. You need to create a SQL *Plus environment variable X and issue the command: X: = CALCTAX (1000);
D. You need to create a SQL *Plus environment variable X and issue the command EXECUTE :X := CALCTAX;
E. You need to create a SQL *Plus environment variable X and issue the command EXECUTE :X := CALCTAX(1000);

Answer: E

16. What happens during the execute phase with dynamic SQL for INSERT, UPDATE, and DELETE operations?

A. The rows are selected and ordered.
B. The validity of the SQL statement is established.
C. An area of memory is established to process the SQL statement.
D. The SQL statement is run and the number of rows processed is returned.
E. The area of memory established to process the SQL statement is released.

Answer: D

Explanation:

All SQL statements have to go through various stages. Some stages may be skipped.

Parse

Every SQL statement must be parsed. Parsing the statement includes checking the statement's syntax and validating the statement, ensuring that all references to objects are correct, and ensuring that the relevant privileges to those objects exist.

Bind

After parsing, the Oracle server knows the meaning of the Oracle statement but still may not have enough information to execute the statement. The Oracle server may need values for any bind variable in the statement. The process of obtaining these values is called binding variables.

Execute

At this point, the Oracle server has all necessary information and resources, and the statement is executed.

Fetch

In the fetch stage, rows are selected and ordered (if requested by the query), and each successive fetch retrieves another row of the result, until the last row has been fetched. You can fetch queries, but not the DML statements.

17. What part of a database trigger determines the number of times the trigger body executes?

A. Trigger type
B. Trigger body
C. Trigger event
D. Trigger timing

Answer: A

18. Examine this code:

CREATE OR REPLACE FUNCTION gen_email_name

(p_first_name VARCHAR2, p_last_name VARCHAR2, p_id NUMBER)

RETURN VARCHAR2

is

v_email_name VARCHAR2(19); BEGIN

v_email_home := SUBSTR(p_first_name, 1, 1) ||

SUBSTR(p_last_name, 1, 7) || '@Oracle.com';

UPDATE employees

SET email = v_email_name WHERE employee_id = p_id; RETURN v_email_name; END;

You run this SELECT statement:

SELECT first_name, last_name gen_email_name(first_name, last_name, 108) EMAIL FROM employees;

What occurs?

A. Employee 108 has his email name updated based on the return result of the function.
B. The statement fails because functions called from SQL expressions cannot perform DML.
C. The statement fails because the functions does not contain code to end the transaction.
D. The SQL statement executes successfully, because UPDATE and DELETE statements are ignoring in stored functions called from SQL expressions.
E. The SQL statement executes successfully and control is passed to the calling environment.

Answer: B

19. Which table should you query to determine when your procedure was last compiled?

A. USER_PROCEDURES
B. USER_PROCS
C. USER_OBJECTS
D. USER_PLSQL_UNITS

Answer: C

20. Examine this code:

CREATE OR REPLACE TRIGGER secure_emp BEFORE LOGON ON employees

BEGIN

IF (TO_CHAR(SYSDATE, 'DY') IN ('SAT', 'SUN')) OR (TO_CHAR(SYSDATE, 'HH24:MI'

NOT BETWEEN '08:00' AND '18:00')

THEN RAISE_APPLICATION_ERROR (-20500, 'You may

insert into the EMPLOYEES table only during business hours.');

END IF; END;

/

What type of trigger is it?

A. DML trigger
B. INSTEAD OF trigger
C. Application trigger
D. System event trigger

E. This is an invalid trigger.

Answer: E

Explanation:

The Triggering Event is incorrect. A User does not LOGON or LOGOFF from a Table. You can't create a BEFORE LOGON or AFTER LOGOFF trigger.

21. Examine this package:

CREATE OR REPLACE PACKAGE discounts IS

g_id NUMBER := 7829;

discount_rate NUMBER := 0.00;

PROCEDURE display_price (p_price NUMBER); END discounts;

/

CREATE OR REPLACE PACKAGE BODY discounts IS

PROCEDURE display_price (p_price NUMBER) IS

BEGIN

DBMS_OUTPUT.PUT_LINE('Discounted   '||
TO_CHAR(p_price*NVL(discount_rate, 1))); END display_price;

BEGIN

/

discount_rate:= 0.10; END discounts;

Which statement is true?

A. The value of DISCOUNT_RATE always remains 0.00 in a session.
B. The value of DISCOUNT_RATE is set to 0.10 each time the package is invoked in a session.
C. The value of DISCOUNT_RATE is set to 1.00 each time the procedure DISPLAY_PRICE is invoked.
D. The value of DISCOUNT_RATE is set to 0.10 when the package is invoked for the first time in a session.

Answer: D

Explanation:

A one-time-only procedure is executed only once, when the package is first invoked within the user session

22. Examine this code:

CREATE OR REPLACE TRIGGER update_emp AFTER UPDATE ON emp

BEGIN

INSERT INTO audit_table (who, dated) VALUES (USER, SYSDATE);

END;

You issue an UPDATE command in the EMP table that results in changing 10 rows.

How many rows are inserted into the AUDIT_TABLE?

A. 1
B. 10
C. None
D. A value equal to the number of rows in the EMP table.

Answer: A

Explanation:

Since the Trigger Type is not specified this Trigger defaults to a FOR EACH STATEMENT Trigger. FOR EACH STATEMENT fire once for the triggering event, therefore one record will be inserted into the audit_table.

23. Examine this package:

CREATE OR REPLACE PACKAGE BB_PACK IS

V_MAX_TEAM_SALARY NUMBER(12,2);

PROCEDURE ADD_PLAYER(V_ID IN NUMBER, V_LAST_NAME VARCHAR2, V_SALARY_NUMBER;

END BB_PACK;

/

CREATE OR REPLACE PACKAGE BODY BB_PACK IS

PROCEDURE UPD_PLAYER_STAT

(V_ID IN NUMBER, V_AB IN NUMBER DEFAULT 4, V_HITS IN NUMBER)

IS BEGIN

UPDATE PLAYER_BAT_STAT

SET AT_BATS = AT_BATS + V_AB, HITS = HITS + V_HITS

WHERE PLAYER_ID = V_ID) COMMIT;

END UPD_PLAYER_STAT;

PROCEDURE ADD_PLAYER

(V_ID IN NUMBER, V_LAST_NAME VARCHAR2, V_SALARY NUMBER) IS

BEGIN

INSERT INTO PLAYER(ID,LAST_NAME,SALARY) VALUES (V_ID, V_LAST_NAME, V_SALARY); UPD_PLAYER_STAT(V_ID,0.0);

END ADD_PLAYER; END BB_PACK;

Which statement will successfully assign $75,000,000 to the V_MAX_TEAM_SALARY variable from within a stand-alone procedure?

A. V_MAX_TEAM_SALARY := 7500000;
B. BB_PACK.ADD_PLAYER.V_MAX_TEAM_SALARY :=75000000;
C. BB_PACK.V_MAX_TEAM_SALARY := 75000000;
D. This variable cannot be assigned a value from outside the package.

Answer: C

Explanation:

To assign a value for a public variable which is declared in the package header, all what you have to do is do user the following syntax : package_name.var_name:=value;

24. There is a CUSTOMER table in a schema that has a public synonym CUSTOMER and you are granted all object privileges on it. You have a procedure PROCESS_CUSTOMER that processes customer information that is in the public synonym CUSTOMER table. You have just created a new table called CUSTOMER within your schema. Which statement is true?

A. Creating the table has no effect and procedure PROCESS_CUSTOMER still accesses data from public synonym CUSTOMER table.
B. If the structure of your CUSTOMER table is the same as the public synonym CUSTOMER table then the procedure PROCESS_CUSTOMER is invalidated and gives compilation errors.
C. If the structure of your CUSTOMER table is entirely different from the public synonym CUSTOMER table then the procedure PROCESS_CUSTOMER successfully recompiles and accesses your CUSTOMER table.

D. If the structure of your CUSTOMER table is the same as the public synonym CUSTOMER table then the procedure PROCESS_CUSTOMER successfully recompiles when invoked and accesses your CUSTOMER table

Answer: D

Explanation:

The procedure will first look in the owner of the procedure schema before looking for the public synonym.

25. Which two statements about packages are true? (Choose two)

A. Both the specification and body are required components of a package.
B. The package specification is optional, but the package body is required.
C. The package specification is required, but the package body is optional.
D. The specification and body of the package are stored together in the database.
E. The specification and body of the package are stored separately in the database.

Answer: C, E

Explanation:

A Package must have a specification. A Package may also have a body but it is not necessary. A Package without a package body are referred to as a bodiless package. If a package specification contains only variables, constants, types, exceptions, and a call specification, the package body is not required. Also, the package specification and body are stored separately in the database.

26. When creating a function in SQL *Plus, you receive this message: "Warning: Function created with compilation errors."

Which command can you issue to see the actual error message?

A. SHOW FUNCTION_ERROR
B. SHOW USER_ERRORS
C. SHOW ERRORS
D. SHOW ALL_ERRORS

Answer: C

Explanation:

The SQL *Plus command SHOW ERRORS or SHOW ERR Command extracts the error information from the USER_ERRORS view

27. Which four triggering events can cause a trigger to fire? (Choose four)

    A. A specific error or any errors occurs.
    B. A database is shut down or started up.
    C. A specific user or any user logs on or off.
    D. A user executes a CREATE or an ALTER table statement.
    E. A user executes a SELECT statement with an ORDER BY clause.
    F. A user executes a JOIN statement that uses four or more tables.

    Answer: A, B, C, D

28. Examine this procedure:

    CREATE OR REPLACE PROCEDURE ADD_PLAYER

    (V_ID IN NUMBER, V_LAST_NAME VARCHAR2) IS

    BEGIN

    INSERT INTO PLAYER (ID,LAST_NAME) VALUES (V_ID, V_LAST_NAME);
    COMMIT;

    END;

    This procedure must invoke the APD_BAT_STAT procedure and pass a parameter.

    Which statement, when added to the above procedure will successfully invoke the UPD_BAT_STAT procedure?

    A. EXECUTE UPD_BAT_STAT(V_ID);
    B. UPD_BAT_STAT(V_ID);

    C. RUN UPD_BAT_STAT(V_ID);
    D. START UPD_BAT_STAT(V_ID);

    Answer: B

    Explanation:

    When invoking a Procedure from within another procedure you omit the EXECUTE. You call the Procedure by specifying the Procedure Name and the argument list and a semi-colon

29. Which statement about triggers is true?

    A. You use an application trigger to fire when a DELETE statement occurs.

B. You use a database trigger to fire when an INSERT statement occurs.

C. You use a system event trigger to fire when an UPDATE statement occurs.

D. You use INSTEAD OF trigger to fire when a SELECT statement occurs.

Answer: B

Explanation:

Database trigger - Fires when a particular event occurs in the database. The events that fire a database trigger are Data events and System events. Data events consist of DML statements (INSERT, UPDATE & DELETE) and DDL statements, such as CREATE or DROP. System Events Comprised of actions that are performed either at the schema level or database level.

30. You want to create a PL/SQL block of code that calculates discounts on customer orders. -This code will be invoked from several places, but only within the program unit ORDERTOTAL.

What is the most appropriate location to store the code that calculates the discounts?

A. A stored procedure on the server.

B. A block of code in a PL/SQL library.

C. A standalone procedure on the client machine.

D. A block of code in the body of the program unit ORDERTOTAL.

E. A local subprogram defined within the program unit ORDERTOTAL.

Answer: E

31. Which type of argument passes a value from a procedure to the calling environment?

A. VARCHAR2

B. BOOLEAN

C. OUT

D. IN

Answer: C

Explanation:

Parameters that are defined with an OUT mode the parameter will pass their value from the procedure back to the calling environment.

32. You create a DML trigger. For the timing information, which is valid with a DML trigger?

A. DURING

B. INSTEAD
C. ON SHUTDOWN
D. BEFORE
E. ON STATEMENT EXECUTION

Answer: D

Explanation:

BEFORE, AFTER and INSTEAD are valid Trigger Timing Events

33. You are about to change the arguments of the CALC_TEAM_AVG function. Which dictionary view can you query to determine the names of the procedures and functions that invoke the CALC_TEAM_AVG function?

A. USER_PROC_DEPENDS
B. USER_DEPENDENCIES
C. USER_REFERENCES
D. USER_SOURCE

Answer: B

Explanation:

The data dictionary view USER_DEPENDENCIES displays information about all direct dependencies within your schema.

34. A CALL statement inside the trigger body enables you to call_.

A. A package.
B. A stored function.
C. A stored procedure.
D. Another database trigger.

Answer: C

35. You need to remove the database trigger BUSINESS_HOUR.

Which command do you use to remove the trigger in the SQL *Plus environment?

A. DROP TRIGGER business_hour;
B. DELETE TRIGGER business_hour;
C. REMOVE TRIGGER business_hour;
D. ALTER TRIGGER business_hour REMOVE;
E. DELETE FROM USER_TRIGGERS WHERE TRIGGER_NAME = 'BUSINESS_HOUR';

Answer: A

Explanation:

To permanently remove a trigger from a database, you can use the DROP TRIGGER statement.

36. How can you migrate from a LONG to a LOB data type for a column?

   A. Use the DBMS_MANAGE_LOB.MIGRATE procedure.
   B. Use the UTL_MANAGE_LOB.MIGRATE procedure.
   C. Use the DBMS_LOB.MIGRATE procedure.
   D. Use the ALTER TABLE command.
   E. You cannot migrate from a LONG to a LOB date type for a column.

Answer: D

37. Examine this procedure:

   CREATE OR REPLACE PROCEDURE INSERT_TEAM

   (V_ID in NUMBER, V_CITY in VARCHAR2 DEFAULT 'AUSTIN', V_NAME in VARCHAR2)

   IS BEGIN

   INSERT INTO TEAM (id, city, name) VALUES (v_id, v_city, v_name);
   COMMIT;

   END

   Which two statements will successfully invoke this procedure in SQL *Plus? (Choose two)

   A. EXECUTE INSERT_TEAM;
   B. EXECUTE INSERT_TEAM(3, V_NAME=>'LONGHORNS',
      V_CITY=>'AUSTIN');
   C. EXECUTE INSERT_TEAM(3, 'AUSTIN','LONGHORNS');
   D. EXECUTE INSERT_TEAM (V_ID := V_NAME :='LONGHORNS',V_CITY :=
      'AUSTIN');
   E. EXECUTE INSERT_TEAM (3, 'LONGHORNS');

Answer: B, C

38. To be callable from a SQL expression, a user-defined function must do what?

   A. Be stored only in the database.
   B. Have both IN and OUT parameters.
   C. Use the positional notation for parameters.
   D. Return a BOOLEAN or VARCHAR2 data type.

Answer: C

Explanation:

Functions called from SQL statements must use positional notation to pass values to the IN parameters.

39. Which two describe a stored procedure? (Choose two)

A. A stored procedure is typically written in SQL.
B. A stored procedure is a named PL/SQL block that can accept parameters.
C. A stored procedure is a type of PL/SQL subprogram that performs an action.
D. A stored procedure has three parts: the specification, the body, and the exception handler part.
E. The executable section of a stored procedure contains statements that assigns values, control execution, and return values to the calling environment.

Answer: B, C

Explanation:

A procedure is a named PL/SQL block that can accept parameters (sometimes referred to as arguments), and be invoked. Generally speaking, you use a procedure to perform an action. A procedure has a header, a declaration section, an executable section, and an optional exception-handling section.

A procedure can be compiled and stored in the database as a schema object.

Procedures promote reusability and maintainability. When validated, they can be used in any number of applications. If the requirements change, only the procedure needs to be updated.

40. Examine this code:

CREATE OR REPLACE PROCEDURE add_dept

(p_name departments.department_name%TYPE DEFAULT 'unknown',

p_loc departments.location_id%TYPE DEFAULT 1700) IS

BEGIN

INSERT INTO departments(department_id, department_name, loclation_id)

VALUES(dept_seq.NEXTVAL,p_name, p_loc); END add_dept;

/

You created the add_dept procedure above, and you now invoke the procedure in SQL *Plus.

Which four are valid invocations? (Choose four)

A. EXECUTE add_dept(p_loc=>2500)
B. EXECUTE add_dept('Education', 2500)
C. EXECUTE add_dept('2500', p_loc =>2500)
D. EXECUTE add_dept(p_name=>'Education', 2500)
E. EXECUTE add_dept(p_loc=>2500, p_name=>'Education')

Answer: A, B, C, E

41. Which three are valid ways to minimize dependency failure? (Choose three)

A. Querying with the SELECT * notification.
B. Declaring variables with the %TYPE attribute.
C. Specifying schema names when referencing objects.
D. Declaring records by using the %ROWTYPE attribute.
E. Specifying package.procedure notation while executing procedures.

Answer: A, B, D

42. Which two does the INSTEAD OF clause in a trigger identify? (Choose two)

A. The view associated with the trigger.
B. The table associated with the trigger.
C. The event associated with the trigger.
D. The package associated with the trigger.
E. The statement level or for each row association to the trigger.

Answer: A, C

Explanation:

INSTEAD OF TRIGGERS are created on views to allow DML statements on an on-updateable view. An INSETED OF Trigger can fire for all three Triggering Events (INSERT, UPDATE and UPDATE).

43. Examine this package:

CREATE OR REPLACE PACKAGE manage_emps IS

tax_rate CONSTANT NUMBER(5,2) := .28;

v_id NUMBER;

PROCEDURE insert_emp (p_deptno NUMBER, p_sal NUMBER);
PROCEDURE delete_emp;

```
PROCEDURE update_emp; FUNCTION calc_tax (p_sal NUMBER) RETURN
NUMBER;

END manage_emps;

/

CREATE OR REPLACE PACKAGE BODY manage_emps IS

PROCEDURE update_sal (p_raise_amt NUMBER) IS

BEGIN

UPDATE emp

SET sal = (sal * p_raise_emt) + sal WHERE empno = v_id;

END;

PROCEDURE insert_emp

(p_deptno NUMBER, p_sal NUMBER) IS

BEGIN

INSERT INTO emp(empno, deptno, sal) VALYES(v_id, p_depntno, p_sal);

END insert_emp; PROCEDURE delete_emp IS

BEGIN

DELETE FROM emp

WHERE empno = v_id; END delete_emp; PROCEDURE update_emp IS

v_sal NUMBER(10, 2);

v_raise NUMBER(10, 2); BEGIN

SELECT sal INTO v_sal FROM emp


WHERE empno = v_id; IF v_sal < 500 THEN v_raise := .05;

ELSIP v_sal < 1000 THEN

v_raise := .07; ELSE

v_raise := .04; END IF;

update_sal(v_raise); END update_emp; FUNCTION calc_tax (p_sal NUMBER)
RETURN NUMBER IS

BEGIN
```

RETURN p_sal * tax_rate; END calc_tax;

END manage_emps;

/

What is the name of the private procedure in this package?

A. CALC_TAX
B. INSERT_EMP
C. UPDATE_SAL
D. DELETE_EMP
E. UPDATE_EMP
F. MANAGE_EMPS

Answer: C

Explanation:

This procedure is not declared in the package specification and therefore it is not public. Constructs declared and defined in the package body are known as private constructs. These constructs are available from inside the package only and cannot be called from outside the package.

44. What can you do with the DBMS_LOB package?

A. Use the DBMS_LOB.WRITE procedure to write data to a BFILE.
B. Use the DBMS_LOB.BFILENAME function to locate an external BFILE.
C. Use the DBMS_LOB.FILEEXISTS function to find the location of a BFILE.
D. Use the DBMS_LOB.FILECLOSE procedure to close the file being accessed.

Answer: D

45. Examine this package:

CREATE OR REPLACE PACKAGE BB_PACK IS

V_MAX_TEAM_SALARY NUMBER(12,2);

PROCEDURE ADD_PLAYER(V_ID IN NUMBER, V_LAST_NAME VARCHAR2, V_SALARY NUMBER);

END BB_PACK;

/

CREATE OR REPLACE PACKAGE BODY BB_PACK IS

V_PLAYER_AVG NUMBER(4,3); PROCEDURE UPD_PLAYER_STAT

V_ID IN NUMBER, V_AB IN NUMBER DEFAULT 4, V_HITS IN NUMBER) IS

BEGIN

UPDATE PLAYER_BAT_STAT

SET AT_BATS = AT_BATS + V_AB, HITS = HITS + V_HITS

WHERE PLAYER_ID = V_ID; COMMIT; VALIDATE_PLAYER_STAT(V_ID); END UPD_PLAYER_STAT;

PROCEDURE ADD_PLAYER

(V_ID IN NUMBER, V_LAST_NAME VARCHAR2, V_SALARY NUMBER) IS

BEGIN

INSERT INTO PLAYER(ID,LAST_NAME,SALARY) VALUES (V_ID, V_LAST_NAME, V_SALARY); UPD_PLAYER_STAT(V_ID,0,0);

END ADD_PLAYER; END BB_PACK

/

Which statement will successfully assign .333 to the V_PLAYER_AVG variable from a procedure outside the package?

A. V_PLAYER_AVG := .333;
B. BB_PACK.UPD_PLAYER_STAT.V_PLAYER_AVG :=.333;
C. BB_PACK.V_PLAYER_AVG :=.333;
D. This variable cannot be assigned a value from outside of the package.

Answer: D

Explanation:

Constructs declared and defined in the package body are private constructs and they can't be invoked outside of the package.

46. Examine this code:

CREATE OR REPLACE PACKAGE comm_package IS

g_comm NUMBER := 10;

PROCEDURE reset_comm(p_comm IN NUMBER); END comm_package;

/

User Jones executes the following code at 9:01am: EXECUTE comm_package.g_comm := 15

User Smith executes the following code at 9:05am: EXECUTE comm_paclage.g_comm := 20

Which statement is true?

A. g_comm has a value of 15 at 9:06am for Smith.
B. g_comm has a value of 15 at 9:06am for Jones.
C. g_comm has a value of 20 at 9:06am for both Jones and Smith.
D. g_comm has a value of 15 at 9:03 am for both Jones and Smith.
E. g_comm has a value of 10 at 9:06am for both Jones and Smith.
F. g_comm has a value of 10 at 9:03am for both Jones and Smith

Answer: B

47. Examine this code:

CREATE OR REPLACE FUNCTION gen_email_name

(p_first_name VARCHAR2, p_last_name VARCHAR2, p_id NUMBER) RETURN VARCHAR2

IS

v_email_name VARCHAR2(19=; BEGIN

v_email_name := SUBSTR(p_first_name, 1, 1) ||

SUBSTR(p_last_name, 1, 7) || '@Oracle.com';

UPDATE employees

SET email = v_email_name WHERE employee_id = p_id; RETURN v_email_name; END;

Which statement removes the function?

A. DROP FUNCTION gen_email_name;
B. REMOVE gen_email_name;
C. DELETE gen_email_name;
D. TRUNCATE gen_email_name;
E. ALTER FUNCTION gen_email_name REMOVE;

Answer: A

Explanation:

Stored functions can be permanently removed from the database by dropping them.

48. Examine this procedure:

CREATE OR REPLACE PROCEDURE UPD_BAT_STAT

(V_ID IN NUMBER DEFAULT 10, V_AB IN NUMBER DEFAULT 4) IS

BEGIN

UPDATE PLAYER_BAT_STAT SET AT_BATS = AT_BATS + V_AB WHERE PLAYER_ID = V_ID; COMMIT;

END;

Which two statements will successfully invoke this procedure in SQL *Plus? (Choose two)

A. EXECUTE UPD_BAT_STAT;
B. EXECUTE UPD_BAT_STAT(V_AB=>10,V_ID=>31);
C. EXECUTE UPD_BAT_STAT(31, 'FOUR','TWO');
D. UPD_BAT_STAT(V_AB=>10,V_ID=>31);
E. RUN UPD_BAT_STAT;

Answer: A, B

49. Examine this code:

CREATE OR REPLACE PROCEDURE audit_action (p_who VARCHAR2)

AS BEGIN

INSERT INTO audit(schema_user) VALUES(p_who); END audit_action;

/

CREATE OR REPLACE TRIGGER watch_it AFTER LOGON ON DATABASE

CALL audit_action(ora_login_user)

/

What does this trigger do?

A. The trigger records an audit trail when a user makes changes to the database.
B. The trigger marks the user as logged on to the database before an audit statement is issued.
C. The trigger invoked the procedure audit_action each time a user logs on to his/her schema and adds the username to the audit table.

D. The trigger invokes the procedure audit_action each time a user logs on to the database and adds the username to the audit table.

Answer: D

Explanation:

This trigger fires after a user connects to a database and inserts a record into the audit table.

50. Which view displays indirect dependencies, indenting each dependency?

A. DEPTREE
B. IDEPTREE
C. INDENT_TREE
D. I_DEPT_TREE

Answer: B

Explanation:

The IDEPTREE displays the indirect dependencies with indentation. No indent is used on the first line for the object being analyzed; a single indent indicates a direct dependency, a double indent represents an indirect dependency.

51. The OLD and NEW qualifiers can be used in which type of trigger?

A. Row level DML trigger
B. Row level system trigger
C. Statement level DML trigger
D. Row level application trigger
E. Statement level system trigger
F. Statement level application trigger

Answer: A

Explanation:

The qualifiers: OLD and: NEW can only be used with row level DML triggers.

52. Which statement is true?

A. Stored functions can be called from the SELECT and WHERE clauses only.
B. Stored functions do not permit calculations that involve database links in a distributed environment.
C. Stored functions cannot manipulate new types of data, such as longitude and latitude.

D. Stored functions can increase the efficiency of queries by performing functions in the query rather than in the application.

Answer: D

Explanation:

User-defined functions increase the efficiency of queries by applying the functions in the query itself. This drastically improves the performance because the query is designed to use the function instead of using the query and functions separately from client-side tools when enforcing application logic.

53. Examine the trigger:

CREATE OR REPLACE TRIGGER Emp_count AFTER DELETE ON Emp_tab

FOR EACH ROW DELCARE

n INTEGER; BEGIN

SELECT COUNT(*) INTO n

FROM Emp_tab;

DBMS_OUTPUT.PUT_LINE(' There are now ' || a || ' employees,');

END;

This trigger results in an error after this SQL statement is entered: DELETE FROM Emp_tab WHERE Empno = 7499;

How do you correct the error?

A. Change the trigger type to a BEFORE DELETE.
B. Take out the COUNT function because it is not allowed in a trigger.

C. Remove the DBMS_OUTPUT statement because it is not allowed in a trigger.
D. Change the trigger to a statement-level trigger by removing FOR EACH ROW.

Answer: D

Explanation:

A mutating table is a table against which a data manipulation statement has been issued and the corresponding trigger on the DML statement is reading from the same table, at the same time. Mutating tables are not valid for statement triggers because statement triggers fire only once for each event and allow the process to complete before the trigger is actually fired. Row triggers can cause a table to mutate because row triggers fire for each row. To correct this problem you change the trigger to a Statement-Level Trigger by removing FOR EACH ROW or by specifying FOR EACH STATEMENT.

54. What is true about stored procedures?

A. A stored procedure uses the DELCLARE keyword in the procedure specification to declare formal parameters.
B. A stored procedure is named PL/SQL block with at least one parameter declaration in the procedure specification.
C. A stored procedure must have at least one executable statement in the procedure body.
D. A stored procedure uses the DECLARE keyword in the procedure body to declare formal parameters.

Answer: C

Explanation:

The executable section must contain at least one executable statement. You can include a NULL keyword to fulfill the need to have at least one executable statement in this section. For example,

BEGIN

NULL;

END

55. Examine this code:

CREATE OR REPLACE PROCEDURE insert_dept (p_location_id NUMBER)

IS

v_dept_id NUMBER(4); BEGIN

INSERT INTO departments

VALUES (5, 'Education', 150, p_location_id); SELECT department_id

INTO v_dept_id FROM employees

WHERE employee_id=99999; END insert_dept;

/

CREATE OR REPLACE PROCEDURE insert_location (p_location_id NUMBER,

p_city VARCHAR2) IS

BEGIN

INSERT INTO locations(location_id, city) VALUES (p_location_id, p_city);
insert_dept(p_location_id);

END insert_location;

/

You just created the departments, the locations, and the employees table. You did not insert any rows. Next you created both procedures.

You new invoke the insert_location procedure using the following command: EXECUTE insert_location (19, 'San Francisco')

What is the result in this EXECUTE command?

A. The locations, departments, and employees tables are empty.
B. The departments table has one row. The locations and the employees tables are empty.
C. The location table has one row. The departments and the employees tables are empty.
D. The locations table and the departments table both have one row. The employees table is empty.

Answer: A

56. The creation of which database objects will cause a DDL trigger to fire? (Choose all that apply)

A. Index
B. Cluster
C. Package

D. Function
E. Synonyms
F. Dimensions
G. Database links

Answer: A, B, C, D, E

Explanation:

DDL triggers fire for clusters, functions, indexes, packages, procedures, roles, sequences, synonyms, tables, tablespaces, triggers, types, views, or users.

57. Which two program declarations are correct for a stored program unit? (Choose two)

A. CREATE OR REPLACE FUNCTION tax_amt (p_id NUMBER) RETURN NUMBER

B. CREATE OR REPLACE PROCEDURE tax_amt (p_id NUMBER) RETURN NUMBER
C. CREATE OR REPLACE PROCEDURE tax_amt (p_id NUMBER, p_amount OUT NUMBER)
D. CREATE OR REPLACE FUNCTION tax_amt (p_id NUMBER) RETURN NUMBER(10,2)
E. CREATE OR REPLACE PROCEDURE tax_amt (p_id NUMBER, p_amount OUT NUMBER(10, 2))

Answer: A, C

58. You need to implement a virtual private database (vpd). In order to have the vpd functionality, a trigger is required to fire when every user initiates a session in the database.

What type of trigger needs to be created?

A. DML trigger
B. System event trigger
C. INSTEAD OF trigger
D. Application trigger

Answer: B

Explanation:

System Event Triggers can be defined to fire at either at the schema level or database level. You can create a trigger that is fired when a user connects to the database. The triggering event in this case is LOGON. This trigger can be created either at the database level or at the schema level. If the trigger is created at the database level, the trigger is fired for all the users that connect to the database. If the trigger is created at the schema level, the trigger is fired when the user that created the trigger connects to the database.

59. You have a row level BEFORE UPDATE trigger on the EMP table. This trigger contains a SELECT statement on the EMP table to ensure that the new salary value falls within the minimum and maximum salary for a given job title. What happens when you try to update a salary value in the EMP table?

A. The trigger fires successfully.
B. The trigger fails because it needs to be a row level AFTER UPDATE trigger.
C. The trigger fails because a SELECT statement on the table being updated is not allowed.

D. The trigger fails because you cannot use the minimum and maximum functions in a BEFORE UPDATE trigger.

Answer: C

Explanation:

This will result in a mutating table. A mutating table is a table against which a data manipulation statement has been issued and the corresponding trigger on the DML statement is reading from the same table, at the same time. To work around this you would need to create a statement level trigger with the SELECT statement and place the values into the package variables. Then the ROW Level Trigger could check the values in the package variables.

60. Examine this code:

CREATE OR REPLACE STORED FUNCTION get_sal

(p_raise_amt NUMBER, p_employee_id employees.employee_id%TYPE)
RETURN NUMBER

IS

v_salaryNUMBER; v_raise NUMBER(8,2); BEGIN

SELECT salary INTO v_salary FROM employees

WHERE employee_id = p_employee_id; v_raise := p_raise_amt * v_salary;
RETURN v_raise;

END;

Which statement is true?

A. This statement creates a stored procedure named get_sal.
B. This statement returns a raise amount based on an employee id.
C. This statement creates a stored function named get_sal with a status of invalid.
D. This statement creates a stored function named get_sal.

E. This statement fails.

Answer: E

Explanation:

This statement will fail. Remove the STORED from CREATE OR REPLACE STORED FUNCTION

61. You need to disable all triggers on the EMPLOYEES table. Which command accomplishes this

    A. None of these commands; you cannot disable multiple triggers on a table in one command.
    B. ALTER TRIGGERS ON TABLE employees DISABLE;
    C. ALTER employees DISABLE ALL TRIGGERS;
    D. ALTER TABLE employees DISABLE ALL TRIGGERS;

Answer: D

Explanation:

You can disable all triggers using the ALTER TABLE command. The syntax to disable or re-enable all triggers on a particular table is:

ALTER TABLE <table name> DISABLE | ENABLE ALL TRIGGERS

62. An internal LOB is__.

    A. A table.
    B. A column that is a primary key.
    C. Stored in the database.
    D. A file stored outside of the database, with an internal pointer to it from a database column.

Answer: C

Explanation:

Internal LOBs are stored inside the database. To access the internal LOBs, Oracle provides the DBMS_LOB package, which uses the locator to access the LOB values.

63. Examine this code:

CREATE OR REPLACE FUNCTION calc_sal(p_salary NUMBER) RETURN NUMBER

IS

v_raise NUMBER(4,2) DEFAULT 1.08; BEGIN

RETURN v_raise * p_salary; END calc_sal;

/

Which statement accurately call the stored function CALC_SAL? (Choose two)

    A. UPDATE employees (calc_sal(salary)) SET salary = salary * calc_sal(salary);

B. INSERT calc_sal(salary) INTO employees WHERE department_id = 60;

C. DELETE FROM employees(calc_sal(salary)) WHERE calc_sal(salary) > 1000;

D. SELECT salary, calc_sal(salary) FROM employees WHERE department_id = 60;

E. SELECT last_name, salary, calc_sal(salary) FROM employees ORDER BY calc_sal(salary);

Answer: D, E

64. This statement fails when executed:

CREATE OR REPLACE TRIGGER CALC_TEAM_AVG AFTER INSERT ON PLAYER

BEGIN

INSERT INTO PLAYER_BATSTAT (PLAYER_ID, SEASON_YEAR,AT_BATS,HITS)

VALUES (:NEW.ID, 1997, 0,0); END;

To which type must you convert the trigger to correct the error?

A. Row
B. Statement
C. ORACLE FORM trigger
D. Before

Answer: A

Explanation:

The qualifiers: OLD and: NEW can only be used with row triggers. If you attempt to create a statement level trigger using the qualifiers, Oracle generates the following error message at compile time:

ORA-01912: ROW keyword expected

65. Examine this code:

CREATE OR REPLACE PROCEDURE audit_emp

(p_id IN emp_empno%TYPE) IS

v_id NUMBER; PROCEDURE log_exec IS

BEGIN

INSERT INTO log_table (user_id, log_delete) VALUES (USER, SYSDATE);

END log_exec;

v_name VARCHAR2(20); BEGIN

DELETE FROM emp

WHERE empno = p_id; log_exec;

SELECT ename, empno INTO v_name, v_id FROM emp

WHERE empno = p_id; END audit_emp;

Why does this code cause an error when compiled?

A. An insert statement is not allowed in a subprogram declaration.
B. Procedure LOG_EXEC should be declared before any identifiers.
C. Variable v_name should be declared before declaring the LOG_EXEC procedure.
D. The LOG_EXEC procedure should be invoked as EXECUTE log_exec with the AUDIT_EMP procedure.

Answer: C

Explanation:

Variables must be declared before declaring any subprograms.

66. Examine this code:

CREATE OR REPLACE PACKAGE metric_converter IS

c_height CONSTRAINT NUMBER := 2.54; c_weight CONSTRAINT NUMBER := .454;

FUNCTION calc_height (p_height_in_inches NUMBER) RETURN NUMBER;

FUNCTION calc_weight (p_weight_in_pounds NUMBER) RETURN NUMBER;

END;

/

CREATE OR REPLACE PACKAGE BODY metric_converter IS

FUNCTION calc_height (p_height_in_inches NUMBER) RETURN NUMBER

IS BEGIN

RETURN p_height_in_inches * c_height; END calc_height;

FUNCTION calc_weight (p_weight_in_pounds NUMBER) RETURN NUMBER

IS BEGIN

RETURN p_weight_in_pounds * c_weight END calc_weight

END metric_converter;

/

CREATE OR REPLACE FUNCTION calc_height (p_height_in_inches NUMBER)

RETURN NUMBER IS

BEGIN

RETURN p_height_in_inches * metric_converter.c_height; END calc_height;

/

Which statement is true?

A. If you remove the package specification, then the package body and the stand alone stored function CALC_HEIGHT are removed.
B. If you remove the package body, then the package specification and the stand alone stored function CALC_HEIGHT are removed.
C. If you remove the package specification, then the package body is removed.
D. If you remove the package body, then the package specification is removed.
E. If you remove the stand alone stored function CALC_HEIGHT, then the METRIC_CONVERTER package body and the package specification are removed.
F. The standalone function CALC_HEIGHT cannot be created because its name is used in a packaged function.

Answer: C

Explanation:

If you remove the package specification, the package body will be removed. To remove the package specification and the package body from the database, you use the following syntax:

DROP PACKAGE ;

The DROP PACKAGE statement removes both the package specification and the package body from the database.

67. What is a condition predicate in a DML trigger?

A. A conditional predicate allows you to specify a WHEN-LOGGING-ON condition in the trigger body.
B. A conditional predicate means you use the NEW and OLD qualifiers in the trigger body as a condition.
C. A conditional predicate allows you to combine several DML triggering events into one in the trigger body.
D. A conditional predicate allows you to specify a SHUTDOWN or STARTUP condition in the trigger body.

Answer: C

Explanation:

A trigger can fire for all three DML statements, INSERT, UPDATE, and DELETE. You can create a single trigger that fires whenever any of the three events occur. You can determine which one of the three DML statements caused the trigger to fire. There three conditional predicates are INSERTING, UPDATING, and DELETING. All three predicates are BOOLEAN values indicating a TRUE or FALSE value in response to the triggering event that fired the trigger. You can check these BOOLEAN values to control processing within the trigger body.

68. Examine this package specification:

CREATE OR REPLACE PACKAGE concat_all IS

v_string VARCHAR2(100);

PROCEDURE combine (p_num_val NUMBER); PROCEDURE combine (p_date_val DATE);

PROCEDURE combine (p_char_val VARCHAR2, p_num_val NUMBER); END concat_all;

/

Which overloaded COMBINE procedure declaration can be added to this package specification?

A. PROCEDURE combine;
B. PROCEDURE combine (p_no NUMBER);
C. PROCEDURE combine (p_val_1 VARCHAR2, p_val_2 NUMBER;
D. PROCEDURE concat_all (p_num_val VARCHAR2, p_char_val NUMBER);

Answer: A

Explanation:

You use the package overloading feature when the same operation is performed using arguments of different types.

69. Local procedure A calls remote procedure B. Procedure B was compiled at 8 A.M. Procedure A was modified and recompiled at 9 A.M. Remote procedure B was later modified and recompiled at 11 A.M. The dependency mode is set to TIMESTAMP. What happens when procedure A is invoked at 1 P.M?

   A. There is no effect on procedure A and it runs successfully.
   B. Procedure B is invalidated and recompiles when invoked.
   C. Procedure A is invalidated and recompiles for the first time it is invoked.
   D. Procedure A is invalidated and recompiles for the second time it is invoked.

Answer: D

Explanation:

When the local procedure is invoked, at run time the Oracle server compares the two time stamps of the referenced remote procedure. If the time stamps are equal (indicating that the remote procedure has not recompiled), the Oracle server executes the local procedure. If the time stamps are not equal (indicating that the remote procedure has recompiled), the Oracle server invalidates the local procedure and returns a runtime error. If the local procedure, which is now tagged as invalid, is invoked a second time, the Oracle server recompiles it before executing, in accordance with the automatic local dependency mechanism. So if a local procedure returns a run-time error the first time that it is invoked, indicating that the remote procedure's time stamp has changed, you should develop a strategy to re-invoke the local procedure.

70. Under which two circumstances do you design database triggers? (Choose two)

   A. To duplicate the functionality of other triggers.
   B. To replicate built-in constraints in the Oracle server such as primary key and foreign key.
   C. To guarantee that when a specific operation is performed, related actions are performed.
   D. For centralized, global operations that should be fired for the triggering statement, regardless of which user or application issues the statement.

Answer: C, D

71. Examine this procedure:

CREATE OR REPLACE PROCEDURE DELETE_PLAYER (V_ID IN NUMBER)

IS BEGIN

DELETE FROM PLAYER WHERE ID = V_ID; EXCEPTION

WHEN STATS_EXITS_EXCEPTION THEN DBMS_OUTPUT.PUT_LINE

('Cannot delete this player, child records exist in PLAYER_BAT_STAT table');

END;

What prevents this procedure from being created successfully?

A. A comma has been left after the STATS_EXIST_EXCEPTION exception.
B. The STATS_EXIST_EXCEPTION has not been declared as a number.
C. The STATS_EXIST_EXCEPTION has not been declared as an exception.
D. Only predefined exceptions are allowed in the EXCEPTION section.

Answer: C

Explanation:

You can't raise an exception that has not been declared.

72. Which command must you issue to allow users to access the UPD_TEAM_STAT trigger on the TEAM table?

A. GRANT SELECT, INSERT, UPDATE, DELETE ON TEAM TO PUBLIC;
B. GRANT SELECT,INSERT,UPDATE,DELETE ON UPD_TEAM_STAT TO PUBLIC;
C. GRANT EXECUTE ON TEAM TO PUBLIC
D. GRANT SELECT, EXECUTE ON TEAM, UPD_TEAM_STAT TO PUBLIC;

Answer: A

73. Which three statements are true regarding database triggers? (Choose three)

A. A database trigger is a PL/SQL block, C, or Java procedure associated with a table, view, schema, or the database.
B. A database trigger needs to be executed explicitly whenever a particular event takes place.
C. A database trigger executes implicitly whenever a particular event takes place.
D. A database trigger fires whenever a data event (such as DML) or system event (such as logon, shutdown) occurs on a schema or database.
E. With a schema, triggers fire for each event for all users; with a database, triggers fire for each event for that specific user.

Answer: A, C, D

74. You create a DML trigger. For the timing information, which are valid with a DML trigger?

A. DURING
B. IN PLACE OF
C. ON SHUTDOWN
D. BEFORE
E. ON STATEMENT EXECUTION

Answer: D

Explanation:

Trigger Timing determines whether the trigger will fire BEFORE or AFTER the DML statement on the table. The BEFORE and AFTER timings are not valid for views. You can only create an INSTEAD OF trigger on a view.

75. Which two statements about the overloading feature of packages are true? (Choose two)

A. Only local or packaged subprograms can be overloaded.
B. Overloading allows different functions with the same name that differ only in their return types.
C. Overloading allows different subprograms with the same number, type and order of parameters.
D. Overloading allows different subprograms with the same name and same number or type of parameters.
E. Overloading allows different subprograms with the same name, but different in either number, type or order of parameters.

Answer: A, E

Explanation:

Only local or packaged subprograms, or type methods, can be overloaded. You cannot overload standalone subprograms.

The Subprograms within the package must have formal parameters that differ in number, data type, or the order of parameters.

76. All users currently have the INSERT privilege on the PLAYER table. You only want your users to insert into this table using the ADD_PLAYER procedure. Which two actions must you take? (Choose two)

A. GRANT SELECT ON ADD_PLAYER TO PUBLIC;
B. GRANT EXECTUE ON ADD_PLAYER TO PUBLIC;
C. GRANT INSERT ON PLAYER TO PUBLIC;
D. GRANT EXECTUE INSERT ON ADD_PLAYER TO PUBLIC;
E. REVOKE INSERT ON PLAYER FROM PUBLIC;

Answer: B, E

Explanation:

You must provide the users with EXECUTE privilege to the procedure. You want to restrict access to the underlying table so you REVOKE the INSERT privilege to PUBLIC.

77. When creating a function, in which section will you typically find the RETURN keyword?

    A. HEADER only
    B. DECLARATIVE
    C. EXECUTABLE and HEADER
    D. DECLARATIVE,EXECUTABLE and EXCEPTION HANDLING

Answer: C

Explanation:

The header of the function contains the RETURN keyword and identifies the data type that needs to be returned to the calling block. The RETURN statement in the executable section of the function performs the actual returning of the value. The header section defines the return data type of the value and the executable section does the actual returning.

78. A dependent procedure or function directly or indirectly references one or more of which four objects? (Choose four)

    A. view
    B. sequence
    C. privilege
    D. procedure
    E. anonymous block
    F. packaged procedure or function

Answer: A, B, D, F

Explanation:

Procedure and function can either directly or indirectly refer to the following objects. Tables, Views, Sequences, Procedures, Functions, Packaged procedures and functions

79. Which three are true regarding error propagation? (Choose three)

    A. An exception cannot propagate across remote procedure calls.

B. An exception raised inside a declaration immediately propagates to the current block.
C. The use of the RAISE; statement in an exception handler reprises the current exception.
D. An exception raised inside an exception handler immediately propagates to the enclosing block.

Answer: A, C, D

Explanation:

Exceptions cannot propagate across remote procedure calls (RPCs). Therefore, a PL/SQL block cannot catch an exception raised by a remote subprogram. For a workaround, see "Defining Your Own Error Messages: Procedure RAISE_APPLICATION_ERROR". To raise an exception you place a RAISE statement in the local exception handler when an exception is raised, the control is passed to the exception-handling section. The control is never transferred back to the executable section after the exception is handled rather it propagates to the enclosing block.

80. Which two tables or views track object dependencies? (Choose two)

A. USER_DEPENDENCIES
B. USER_IDEPTREE
C. IDEPTREE
D. USER_DEPTREE
E. USER_DEPENDS

Answer: A, C

Explanation:

The data dictionary view USER_DEPENDENCIES displays information about all direct dependencies within your schema. The IDEPTREE View displays indirect dependencies in an indented format.

81. Examine the trigger heading:

CREATE OR REPLACE TRIGGER salary_check BEFORE UPDATE OF sal, job ON emp

FOR EACH ROW

Under which condition does this trigger fire?

A. When a row is inserted into the EMP table.
B. When the value of the SAL or JOB column in a row is updated in the EMP table.

C. When any column other than the SAL and JOB columns in a row are updated in the EMP table.

D. Only when both values of the SAL and JOB columns in a row are updated together in the EMP table.

Answer: B

Explanation:

The triggering event is based on an UPDATE of the SAL or the JOB column in the EMP Table.

82. You have an AFTER UPDATE row-level on the table EMP. The trigger queries the EMP table and inserts the updating user's information into the AUDIT_TABLE. What happens when the user updates rows on the EMP table?

A. A compile time error occurs.

B. A runtime error occurs. The effect of trigger body and the triggering statement are rolled back.

C. A runtime error occurs. The effect of trigger body is rolled back, but the update on the EMP table takes place.

D. The trigger fires successfully. The update on the EMP table occurs, and data is inserted into theAUDIT_TABLE table.

E. A runtime error occurs. The update on the EMP table does not take place, but the insert into the AUDIT_TABLE occurs.

Answer: B

Explanation:

This results in a mutating table. A mutating table is a table against which a data manipulation statement has a corresponding trigger on the DML statement is reading from the same table. When a trigger encounters a mutating table, a runtime error occurs, the effects of the trigger body and triggering statement are rolled back, and control is returned to the user or application.

83. The add_player, upd_player_stat, and upd_pitcher_stat procedures are grouped together in a package. A variable must be shared among only these procedures. Where should you declare this variable?

A. In the package body.

B. In a database trigger.

C. In the package specification.

D. In each procedure's DECLARE section, using the exact same name in each.

Answer: A

Explanation:

You want to declare this variable in the package body before the procedures so that it may be shared among all of the procedure. If it was declared in the package specification it would be accessible outside of the package.

84. You disabled all triggers on the EMPLOYEES table to perform a data load. Now, you need to enable all triggers on the EMPLOYEES table. Which command accomplished this?

    A. You cannot enable multiple triggers on a table in one command.
    B. ALTER TRIGGERS ON TABLE employees ENABLE;
    C. ALTER employees ENABLE ALL TRIGGERS;
    D. ALTER TABLE employees ENABLE ALL TRIGGERS;

Answer: D

85. When creating stored procedures and functions, which construct allows you to transfer values to and from the calling environment?

    A. local variables
    B. arguments
    C. Boolean variables
    D. Substitution variables

Answer: B

Explanation:

Arguments declared in the parameter list of the subprogram are called formal parameters. The MODE determines whether the values can be transferred to the calling environment OUT & IN OUT or from the calling Environment IN & IN OUT.

86. Examine this code:

CREATE OR REPLACE FUNCTION gen_email_name (p_first VARCHAR2, p_last VARCHAR2)

RETURN VARCHAR2 IS

v_email_name VARCHAR (19) ; BEGIN

v_email_bame := SUBSTR(p_first, 1, 1) ||

SUBSRE(p_last, 1, 7) || RETURN v_email_name; END

/

Which two statements are true?

A. This function is invalid.
B. This function can be used against any table.
C. This function cannot be used in a SELECT statement.
D. This function can be used only if the two parameters passed in are not bull values.
E. This function will generate a string based on 2 character values passed into the function.
F. This function can be used only on tables where there is a p_first and p_last column.

Answer: D, E

87. Examine the code examples. Which one is correct?

A. CREATE OR REPLACE TRIGGER authorize_action BEFORE INSERT ON EMPLOYEES
CALL log_exectution;
/
B. CREATE OR REPLACE TRIGGER authorize_action BEFORE EMPLOYEES INSERT
CALL log_exectution;
C. CREATE OR REPLACE TRIGGER authorize_action BEFORE EMPLOYEES INSERT
CALL log_exectution;
D. CREATE OR REPLACE TRIGGER authorize_action CALL log_exectution;
BEFORE INSERT ON EMPLOYEES;

Answer: A

88. You need to create a DML trigger. Which five pieces need to be identified? (Choose five)

A. Table
B. DML event
C. Trigger body
D. Package body
E. Package name
F. Trigger name
G. System event
H. Trigger timing

Answer: A, B, C, F, H

89. The add_player procedure inserts rows into the PLAYER table. Which command will show this directory dependency?

A. SELECT * FROM USER_DEPENDENCIES WHERE REFERENCD NAME = ' PLAYER ';
B. SELECT * FROM USER DEPENDENCIES WHERE REFERENCD NAME = ' ADD PLAYER ';
C. SELECT * FROM USER_DEPENDENCIES WHERE TYPE = 'DIR' ;
D. SELECT * FROM USER DEPENDENCIES WHERE REFERENCD NAME = ' TABLE ';

Answer: A

Explanation:

The REFERENCED_NAME Column displays the name of the referenced object. If you specify Player in the Referenced name column all objects that reference the PLAYER Table (Direct Dependencies) will be displayed.

90. When using a packaged function in a query, what is true?

A. The COMMIT and ROLLBACK commands are allowed in the packaged function.
B. You cannot use packaged functions in a query statement.
C. The packaged function cannot execute an INSERT, UPDATE, or DELETE statement against the table that is being queried.
D. The packaged function can execute and INSERT, UPDATE, or DELETE statement against the table that is being queried if it is used in a subquery.
E. The packaged function can execute an INSERT, UPDATEM or DELETE statement against the table that is being queried if the pragma RESTRICT REFERENCE is used.

Answer: C

Explanation:

A function, stand-alone or package can't execute DML (INSERT, UPDATE & DELETE) against the table that is being queried. This will result in a mutating table and generate a runtime error.

91. You have a table with the following definition:

CREATE TABLE long_tab (id NUMBER)

long_col LONG)

You need to convert the LONG_COL column from a LONG data type to a LOB data type. Which statement accomplish this task?

A. ALTER TABLE long_tab MODIFY (LONG_COL CLOB);
B. EXECUTE dbms_lob.migrate(long_tab, long_col, clob)

C. EXECUTE dbms_manage.lob.migrate(long_tab, long_col, clob)
D. EXECUTE utl_lob.migrate(long_tab, long_col, clob)

E. EXECUTE utl_manage_lob.migrate(long_tab, long_col, clob)

Answer: A

92. Why do you use an INSTEAD OF trigger?

A. To perform clean up actions when ending a user session.
B. To insert data into a view that normally does not accept inserts.
C. To insert into an audit table when data is updated in a sensitive column.
D. To modify data in which the DML statement has been issued against an inherently non-updateable view.

Answer: D

Explanation:

An INSTEAD OF trigger is used to perform a DML activity on the underlying tables of a view that is inherently non-updatable.

93. When using a PL/SQL stored package, how is a side effect defined?

A. changes only to database tables
B. changes only to packaged public variables defined in a package body
C. changes only to packaged public variables defined in a package specification
D. changes to database tables or packaged public variables defined in a package body
E. changes to database tables or packaged variables defined in a package specification

Answer: E

94. Which two statements about functions are true? (Choose two.)

A. A function must have a return statement in its body to execute successfully
B. Client-side functions can be used in SOL statements
C. A stored function that is called from a SOL statement can return a value of any PL/SOL variable data type

D. From SOL*Plus, a function can be executed by giving the command EXECUTE function name;

E. A stored function increases efficiency of queries by performing functions on the server rather than in the application

Answer: A, E

95. Examine this code

CREATE OR REPLACE PROCEDURE load bfile (p_flle_loc IN VARCHAR2) IS

V_file BFILE;

v_filename VARCHAR2(16); CURSOR emp_cursor IS SELECT employee_id FROM employees

WHERE Job_id = 'IT_PROG' FROM UPDATE

BEGIN

FOR emp_record IN emp_cursor LOOP
v_filename:=emp_record.emplyee_id||;GIF';
V_file:=BFILENMAE(p_file_loc,v_filename); END LOOP;

END;

/

What does the BFILENAME function do?

A. It reads data from an external BFILE
B. It checks for the existence of an external BFILE
C. It returns a BFILE locator that is associated with a physical LOB binary file on the server's file system
D. It creates a directory object for use with the external BFILEs

Answer: C

Explanation:

In Oracle/PLSQL, the BFILENAME function returns a BFILE locator for a physical LOB binary file.

96. Consider this scenario

A procedure X references a view Y that is based on a table Z. Which two statements are true? (Choose two.)

A. Y is a referenced object
B. Z is a direct dependent of X
C. Y is a direct dependent of X

D. Y is an indirect dependent of X
E. Y is an indirect dependent of Z
F. Z is an indirect dependent of Y

Answer: A, C

97. Which two statements about object dependencies are accurate? (Choose two.)

A. When referencing a package procedure or function from a stand-alone procedure or function, if the package specification changes, the package body remains valid but the stand-alone procedure becomes invalid
B. When referencing a package procedure or function from a stand-alone procedure or function, if the package body changes and the package specification does not change, the stand-alone procedure referencing a package construct remains valid.
C. When referencing a package procedure or function from a stand-alone procedure or function, if the package body changes and the package specification does not change, the stand-alone procedure referencing a package construct becomes invalid
D. When referencing a package procedure or function from a stand-alone procedure or function, If the package specification changes, the stand-alone procedure referencing a package construct as well as the package body become invalid

Answer: B, D

98. You need to create a trigger to ensure that information in the EMP table is only modified during business hours, Monday to Friday from 9:00am to 500pm Which types of trigger do you create? (Choose two.)

A. row level AFTER INSERT OR UPDATE OR DELETE ON EMP
B. row level BEFORE INSERT OR UPDATE OR DELETE ON EMP
C. statement level AFTER INSERT OR UPDATE OR DELETE ON EMP
D. statement level BEFORE INSERT OR UPDATE OR DELETE ON EMP

Answer: B, D

99. Which statement is true about removing packages?

A. You must remove the package body first
B. Removing a package specification removes the body too
C. Removing the package body removes the specification too
D. You must remove both the package body and the specification separately
E. Removing a package specification removes all standalone stored functions named in the specification

Answer: B

100. You want to create procedures, functions and packages which privilege do you need?

    A. EXECUTE CODE object privilege
    B. CREATE ANY CODE object privilege
    C. CREATE PACKAGE system privilege
    D. CREATE PROCEDURE system privilege
    E. CREATE FUNCTION, CREATE PROCEDURE, CREATE PACKAGE system privileges

Answer: D

Explanation:

The privilege CREATE PROCEDURE gives the grantee the right to create procedures, functions, and packages within their schema. This privilege does not give the right to drop or alter the program constructs.

www.ingramcontent.com/pod-product-compliance
Lightning Source LLC
Chambersburg PA
CBHW061044050326
40689CB00012B/2967